JESUIT GENERALS

A GLIMPSE INTO
A FORGOTTEN CORNER

JESUIT GENERALS

A GLIMPSE INTO
A FORGOTTEN CORNER

THOMAS E. ZEYEN, S.J.

Scranton: The University of Scranton Press

Library of Congress Cataloging-in-Publication Data

Zeyen, Thomas E., 1923-
 Jesuit generals : a glimpse into a forgotten corner / by Thomas E. Zeyen.
  p. cm.
 Includes bibliographical references.
 ISBN 1-58966-071-4 (pbk).
 1. Jesuits—Biography. 2. Jesuits—History. I. Title.
 BX3755Z49 2003
271'.53022—dc22   2003064545

Distribution:

University of Scranton Press
Chicago Distribution Center
11030 S. Langley
Chicago IL 60628

PRINTED IN THE UNITED STATES OF AMERICA

CONTENTS

PREFACE

As a librarian I have become painfully aware that there are many books which have been written that serve little purpose or none at all, save for the convenience of putting the authors' thoughts into print. There are some whose pages have never been cut and others that are in prime condition testifying to their lack of use and handling.

Perhaps with this little volume I'm adding to a librarian's woes by taking up precious space on his shelves. For this I beg his forbearance.

When I got the idea of writing this book, giving some exposure to the Generals of the Society of Jesus, I had been struck by the ignorance some Jesuits (many?) have of their antecedents. I seemed to have discovered that the past Generals are a forgotten group and, as a group, should not and must not be forgotten, not only for the sacrifices they made for the Society, but, also, for the confidence the Society itself placed in them by electing them to its highest office. I was spurred on in the research required by finding out that two Generals were taken to Spain for burial and years later their remains were incinerated when their burial place was burned to the ground. One other was buried outside Rome up in Tuscany where the Curia was located at the time of his death.

I have written so that these names will not go into oblivion, that whoever may read these pages will not let this corner of Jesuit History be forgotten and that these men will not lie in their graves "unwept, unhonored and unsung."

No one ever does anything without assistance and this attempt has had the help of fellow Jesuits, whose encouragement, reading of the proofs and the solving for me of some of the mysteries of the computer have made this book possible. They are Fathers Michael Pastizzo, Robert Hurd and Bernard Hall. Were it not for them this volume would not have found an interested and curious readership.

I would also like to acknowledge the information given by the Archivists of the Jesuit Curia and of the Northern Belgian Province in Leuven (Heverlee).

Ignatius Loyola S.J. | I | Præp. Gen. | Span.

IGNATIUS LOYOLA
FIRST GENERAL
(1541-1556)

The basic details of the life of St. Ignatius are so well known by everyone acquainted with the Society of Jesus, that it is superfluous to give them in this book. However, since he was the First General of the Society and this is an account of the "Generals" it seems that this is where we should begin.

Inigo (he changed his name to the Latin form "Ignatius" when he was a student in Paris in 1537) was the last of eleven children of Beltram Yañez de Oñaz y Loyola and Marina Saenz de Licona. He was born in the small castle of Loyola in Axpeizia, Guipuzcoa, the Basque Province of Spain and baptized in the local church where the fact is recorded at the font.

His mother died when he was very young and he grew up mothered by the wife of an older brother. When he was 16 his father died and Inigo was sent to the royal court to learn to be a gentleman worthy of his noble family. Later he entered the army as an officer and distinguished himself for his courage, leadership, and military knowledge.

At the time, the French army was attacking the army of Navarre and Inigo led his Navarese comrades in the defense of the walls of Pamplona in Northern Spain. Alas, a cannon ball struck his right knee and shattered it. With their brave officer disabled the battle was lost and Inigo was carried back to Loyola on a litter to recover or to die.

Doctors tried every means known at the time to straighten the leg, but with no success so that for the remainder of his life he walked with a limp, one leg shorter than the other.

During his long convalescence, to while away the time, he took to reading the Lives of the Saints and the Life of Christ by Ludolf of Saxony, because of the dearth of romantic books on the castle shelves.

This spiritual reading brought about his conversion from a soldier, vain and proud, to a young man attracted to a life of sacrifice and to the service of God.

When he was sufficiently well convalesced he left the castle and went on a pilgrimage to some of the famous shrines in northern Spain— Monserrat, Manresa, and Aránzazu—where he determined to become a world pilgrim and to go to the Holy Land to preach Christ to whom he was now devoted. While at Manresa he spent his time in a cave in

1

prayer, fasting and writing down the spiritual lights that came to him from God.

In 1522 he went to Venice from where he embarked on a cargo ship bound for the Holy Land. After three months there, he was advised by the Franciscans to return home for more practical training and he, himself, realized that he was not properly equipped to preach, so he returned to Venice still determined to prepare himself to return to the Holy Land.

In 1524 he returned to Spain and to the classroom where he sat among much younger students picking up the knowledge that he had previously not thought necessary. He studied in Barcelona, Alcala, and Salamanca and then felt he was ready to study at the University of Paris.

So, it was off to Paris in 1528 where his intelligence, common sense, and holy zeal attracted other students to be his companions. Among these was another Spaniard, Francis Xavier.

They decided to band together and live their lives in common to which they vowed to do in a small chapel of a convent on the slope of Montmartre, a Paris suburb.

They wanted the approval of the Pope for their way of life and their new venture, so they set out for Rome. In Venice on June 24, 1531 they were ordained priests, but Ignatius decided to put off his First Mass until he got to Rome. There in the Basilica of Santa Maria Maggiore he celebrated his first Mass at the altar of the Crib on Christmas Day, 1538. Ignatius and his companions, now calling themselves the "Companions of Jesus" decided to establish their group—or Company—as an order of Priests to teach, preach, and to go to the missions. So, Ignatius took to writing up their plan, their goals and how to accomplish them, which they called the "Constitutions" and submitted an outline of them to Pope Paul III on September 27, 1540, who approved them and gave his Blessing to the newly founded order.

In the next year the Companions assembled to choose one of their number as their leader. On April 19, 1541 they unanimously—and not surprisingly—elected Ignatius as their leader whom they would call "General," in some way a reference to seeing themselves as soldiers of Christ and his Church. The election of Ignatius as General made him the first of a long line through many vicissitudes to the 29th General today.

They formalized their vows in the chapel of the Blessed Sacrament in the Basilica of St. Paul's outside the Walls on April 22 in front of an ancient mosaic image of Our Lady which is still in the same chapel.

For the next 15 years Ignatius was at the head of his little band of Apostles, preaching in the piazzas of Rome and ministering to the poor, their numbers continuing to grow. Improving the Constitutions and guiding his little Company, to and from his rooms at the Jesuit residence he had a constant stream of new recruits and spiritual children. He sent Francis Xavier to India and others to cities of Italy. He kept improving on the Constitutions, rewriting his "Spiritual Exercises" and finding spare moments to dictate the earliest experiences of his spiritual growth for the encouragement of those who would follow him in this Society.

In 1566 after an illness of some months and after a short attempt at convalescence at the Jesuit country Villa, Ignatius was brought home where he died peacefully in his room early in the morning on July 31 at the Gesù. At his death the Society had grown to over 1,000 companions. His bones were laid to rest first in the church and now repose in the Shrine of the altar dedicated to him in the Gesù church in Rome.

DIEGO LAINEZ S.J. | II | PRÆP. GEN. | SPAN.

DIEGO LAINEZ
SECOND GENERAL
(1558-1565)

D iego was born in 1512 at Almazan, Castile in Spain. In 1534 he became one of Ignatius' first companions at the University of Paris. He had studied the humanities at Soria and Sigüenza and Alcala in Spain, but felt the need of the broadening effects which could be received at the University of Paris. He had found more than he had expected when he encountered his fellow-student Ignatius of Loyola, a fellow Spaniard and one who already had a reputation for spiritual direction. After making the Spiritual Exercises under the direction of Ignatius, Diego gave himself completely and whole-heartedly to the little group who had formed around Ignatius. With them he pronounced his vows with six others in the little chapel of a convent on Montmartre and would remain a close companion and collaborator of Ignatius for the rest of his life. With the group he was ordained to the priesthood in Venice while on the way to Rome and later, with them, pronounced his formal vows of Poverty, Chastity, and Obedience in the Chapel of Our Lady in St. Paul's basilica in Rome. By his long association and by the confidence Ignatius had in him, he was trusted with positions of authority. Ignatius depended upon Lainez for help in areas where he, himself, did not have the time or no longer had the endurance. Lainez was posted to the Council of Trent at the request of the Pope himself and as a very prominent theologian was referred to by the Pope as one of the most outstanding diplomats and churchmen of his time.

When Ignatius took sick and finally died, Jesuits in Rome had to assemble and reassess their effectiveness and what the future would hold for them with Ignatius no longer there to advise and guide them. Because of politics and national rivalries, it was two years before the Fathers could be assembled for the meeting they would call a "Congregation." When the day arrived for the assembly where they would discern in prayer and reflection who of their number should take over the authority and burdens that Ignatius, the 1st General, had left behind, the Companions assembled in what is known as the First General Congregation, in the room where Father Ignatius had died. It was a small room, but could easily accommodate the twenty fathers who had to make this momentous decision for the early Company of Jesus. The congregation was held between June 19 and September 10, 1558 and Lainez, only 46 years old at the time, was elected by thirteen votes out of the 20.

The term of his Generalate lasted for six years and six months, from July 2, 1558 until January 19, 1565. He continued faithfully the line traced out by Ignatius because he knew the mind of Ignatius so well.

When he died on January 19, 1565 he was almost 53 years old having spent his time as General in consolidating the Constitutions as written by Ignatius.

The Jesuits throughout Spain requested that his body be sent back to his home to rest among them as encouragement and remembrance. It was so done and his body was interred in the Jesuit Church in Madrid. There his bones rested for almost four hundred years until in 1930 when civil unrest, anti-Catholic sentiment and Masonic influences in the Spain of those years preceding the Spanish Civil War of the mid-thirties, the Jesuit church was torched by a mob and it burned to the ground. What remained of Lainez' bones—only a handful of ashes—were re-interred in the south wall of the present Jesuit Church on Maldonado, where they rest today behind a plaque attesting to their authenticity and the place once held by Lainez in the Society of Jesus.

FRANCISCO BORGIA S.J. | III | PRÆP. GEN. | SPAN.

FRANCISCO BORGIA
THIRD GERNEAL
(1565-1572)

The Duke of Gandia in Spain, who was destined to become the third General of the Jesuits, was born in Gandia, Spain, on October 28, 1510 to Juan and Juana of the high nobility in those times of Spain's glory under Charles V and Philip II. Elizabeth was on the throne of England and Shakespeare was blossoming as one of the greatest playwrights of all time.

The Third Duke had inherited large estates and numerous honors which his illustrious forebears, both famous and infamous, through their good services bequeathed him. Francis' mother Donna Juana was the granddaughter of Ferdinand V, King of Aragon and though the Borgia line was full of scamps and scoundrels, the father and mother of Francis were good Christians. Francis' tutor was an ecclesiastic chosen by his mother and the boy grew up pious, though with all the skills expected of the scion of a noble family. He could not only ride and fence with great skill, but one of his favorite sports was falconry. Besides physical sports, he was a competent musician and as a boy gave little sermons to the good Poor Clare Sisters of which his aunts were members in the local convent. He was intelligent in his studies and was a sportsman with many skills. When he was ten his mother died and he was sent from one relative to the other to polish his character. They all wanted some part in the education of this heir to the Dukedom of Gandia. For the beginning of his royal attachments he became a page at the Court of Catherine, the sister of Charles V. Because of his outstanding pedigree he contracted a marriage with Leonor de Castro, the favorite Lady-in-waiting to the Empress. Despite the fact that it was, more or less, an arranged marriage, Francis was genuinely in love with Leonor by whom he had eight sons.

When the Empress Isabella, in whose service he found himself, died he was chosen by her Will for the honor of accompanying her remains to her burial.

On June 26, 1539 he was appointed Viceroy of Catalonia and at his father's death on December 17, 1542 he claimed his inheritance and rights as successor to the Dukedom.

During his term in Barcelona he first came into contact with the Jesuits and liked what he saw. He built for them a College which Pope Paul IV elevated to the rank of a university in 1547.

9

In 1546 his wife suddenly died and Francis, by this time a close friend, admirer, and collaborator of the Jesuits of Catalonia, secretly petitioned admittance into the Society. He made his solemn profession on February 1, 1548 but continued to wear secular dress in order to administer his estates and to settle the affairs of his children. He studied Theology at the new University he had founded and received a Doctor of Divinity degree on August 20, 1550. He immediately undertook a pilgrimage to Rome in order to arrange with Ignatius for his open and official entrance into the Society. On May 23, 1551 he was ordained at Oñate and said his first Mass at Loyola on August 1. He preached and taught catechism in the Basque province during which he performed severe corporal penances. He remained in the service of the king and assisted Queen Juana in her last illness. After the queen had died and Charles had abdicated to retire to a monastery, he often called upon Francis for advice not only on spiritual matters, but also on matters of State.

Borgia was eventually called to Rome by Pope Paul IV in 1561 and three years later was appointed Vicar General and Assistant General of the Jesuits for Spain and Portugal.

When Diego Lainez died in 1565 Borgia was chosen General on July 2 of that year at the Society's Second General Congregation by 23 votes out of 31.

During his 7 years as General, the Society continued to grow. He established new missions in the New World. He re-founded the German College in Rome to prepare missionaries to return and re-evangelize their own country, in great part lost to the Protestants. Other Colleges were established in France and Poland and the Roman College received his special consideration in the appointment of professors. The Gesù Church and the Novitiate of St. Andrea just behind the Quirinal Palace were established.

He died on September 30, 1572 and his remains, like those of his predecessor, were placed in the little church of the Curia. At the time of his beatification, his nephew, the Duke of Lerma, petitioned to have his body sent to Spain and interred along with Lainez in Madrid. The request was granted, and the two Generals were entombed side by side in the Jesuit Church, but both remains met the same fate when the Jesuit Church was burned to the ground in the political unrest of the early 1930s.

His few ashes which remained were then re-interred in the south wall of the present Jesuit Church and identified by a plaque giving the important dates and the office he had held in the Society for 7 years.

Everard Mercurian S.J. | IV | Præp. Gen. | Belg.

EVERARD MERCURIAN
FOURTH GENERAL
1573–1580

He was born in Marcourt in the Belgian Province of Luxembourg in 1514 in the South-East corner of Belgium. He was of humble origin and from a place of no importance in the secular world. He went to the University of Paris, was ordained and became a parish priest. He became acquainted with Jesuits at the University and on September 8, 1548 he entered the Society in Belgium. Successively he became Visitor of the German Province and later Provincial of the Lower German Province and lastly the German Assistant in 1565.

After the death of Borgia when the Third General Congregation was about to convene, Pope Gregory XIII (Boncompagni), a good friend of the Society, expressed his desire that the delegates elect a General who was not a Spaniard. The First three had been Spaniards and there was some concern that "New Christians"—converted Jews or Muslims—might enter into the mainstream of the Society. Polanco, a close associate of Father Ignatius, was a Spaniard and was suspected of having a racial background that would not be acceptable. So, the Pope suggested that someone from another country be chosen as General, even though Polanco would have been the natural choice. The Fathers of the Congregation voted 27 out of 47 on April 23, 1573 for the election of Everard Mercurian, a Belgian. It was a choice which pleased the Pope because Mercurian was a good friend, a non-Spaniard, and besides, there was no chance of his having tainted blood.

During his seven years and three months as General, he published a Summary of the Constitutions and made a revision of the Rules. From his friend Gregory the Society received charge of the English College and Gregory's beneficence to the Roman College was much appreciated. During this time, too, Polanco traveled the length and breadth of Europe making a census of the Society's activities and of its men. When it was finally finished it filled six large volumes and gave a detailed account of the progress the Society had made from 1537 until the death of Ignatius.

Mercurian died, a martyr of charity, during the influenza epidemic of 1580 while visiting the sick in their homes. He was 66 at the time of his death and was buried in the Church of St. Andrea al Quirinale, at that time the church of the Novitiate. Later on, his remains were transferred to the Ossuary in the crypt of the Gesù. At the time of his death the Society had grown to 5,000 members in 21 provinces.

CLAUDIO AQUAVIVA S.J. | V | PRÆP. GEN | ITAL.

CLAUDIO AQUAVIVA
FIFTH GENERAL
1581-1615

Claudio was born in Naples the youngest son of Giovanni Antonio Donato d'Aragona, the Duke of Atri in the year 1543. He studied Jurisprudence in Perugia planning a promising career in the Papal service. When he finished his studies Pope Pius IV appointed him a Papal Chamberlain, but Claudio decided to enter the Society of Jesus with which he had become acquainted through his friendship with Francis Borgia and Juan de Polanco. He was 24 years old when he entered the Society in 1567.

After his Novitiate and a short period teaching Philosophy he became the Rector, then the Superior, at Naples, stepping next into the office of Provincial of Naples and the Provincial of Rome.

When the 4th General Congregation was called for February 7, 1581 after the death of Mercurian, Aquaviva was elected unanimously by the 57 votes of all the delegates. He was only 37 years old and had been in the Society only 14 years.

During his 33 years and 11 months as General there is understandably a long list of his accomplishments and interests. The size of the Society had tripled from 5,000 to 13,000, schools from 124 to 372 and Provinces from 21 to 32. It was during his generalate that the famous Jesuit Missions in Paraguay were set up. He actively promoted the Missions in Japan, England, Germany, France, Flanders, and Spain. He was very cognizant of the cultural problems the Jesuit missionaries faced in distant mission lands. He encouraged the setting up of Sodalities for students and alumni of Jesuit Colleges and he tried to moderate the upheaval brought on by the theories of Galileo. He offered to Gregory XIII many of the most competent Jesuit scientists to set up the new dating of the Calendar on October 15, 1582 and entrusted the task to the most eminent of all, Christopher Clavius, the most distinguished mathematician of the time. He had appointed Robert Bellarmine Rector of the Roman College and was present when the Church of the Gesù was finally finished and was also present at its consecration in 1583. It was he who approved the entrance of Aloysius Gonzaga into the Society on November 25, 1585.

After these many accomplishments and long years of governance of the Society, he died at the age of 62 on January 31, 1615. At first he was buried in the Church of St. Ignatius, but was later transferred to the Ossuary in the crypt of the Gesù.

15

MUTIUS VITELLESCHI S.J | VI | PRÆP. GEN. | ITAL.

MUTIUS VITELLESCHI
SIXTH GENERAL
(1615-1645)

He was born in 1563 in Venice, that glorious jewel of the Adriatic, not far from Bologna where the Council of Trent was in full session, having transferred from Trent for lack of space. In 1583, at the age of 20, he entered the Society whose reputation was enormous with a membership of over 10,000 and more than 400 colleges throughout Europe. After his training in the Society he was put to teaching Philosophy and Theology, but after 10 years he became Rector of the English College, which possibly influenced him later on as General to make England a separate Province and to establish a Novitiate in London. Eventually he became the Provincial of Rome and then of Naples and in 1608 became the Assistant for Italy.

After the death of Aquaviva the 7th General Congregation was called for November 5, 1615 and would last until January 6, 1616. On November 15, 1615, Vitelleschi at 51 years old was elected the 6th General of the Society.

He has often been criticized for his mild rule, still the Society grew to over 16,000 members and 35 provinces. In his governance he stayed within the guidelines of St. Ignatius and proceeded with determination and gentleness. He had established the tenure of Superiors and how often there should be a General Congregation.

After 29 years and 3 months as General he died at the venerable age of 82 on February 9, 1645 and his remains were placed in the crypt of the Gesù.

VINCENT CARAFFA S.J. | VII | PRÆP. GEN. | ITAL.

VINCENT CARAFFA
SEVENTH GENERAL
(1645–1649)

To the noble and venerable Caraffa family of Naples on May 9, 1585 a son was born whom they named Vincent. He was the third son of the Duke of Andria. Francis Geronimo the Jesuit of southern Italy who had established a reputation as a giver of popular parish missions, found a ready and capable collaborator in the young Vincent.

Under the influence of Francis, Vincent entered the Society and after ordination taught Philosophy and gave popular missions under the tutelage of Francis. He directed a group of Nobles in doing social work, so that it became the central point of the whole region for social action and charitable work in the Naples area. By the time Vitelleschi died in 1645, Caraffa had become Provincial of Naples and the 8th General Congregation was called to convene on November 21, 1645. The 61-year-old Neapolitan noble, Vincent Caraffa, was elected to be its 7th General with 52 votes out of 88.

His attraction for social work never left him and as General he was known for his charity to the sick and poor, evidently in the footsteps of Ignatius, himself. During the plague and famine experienced in Rome in the years 1648–1649, Caraffa, himself, became personally involved in feeding the hungry and caring for the poor and plague-stricken. In 1624 he had made a vow to seize every opportunity to assist the sick and lowly. Thus occupied for several months, he, himself, contracted the plague from those he had served so selflessly. After a mere 3 years and 5 months as General he died on June 8, 1649. He has been recognized for his holiness and he has left behind writings in Spiritual Direction, written under the pseudonym Luigi Sidereo. His holy remains were devoutly laid in the ossuary in the crypt of the Gesù.

Francisco Piccolomini S.J. | VIII | Præp. Gen. | Ital.

FRANCISCO PICCOLOMINI
EIGHTH GENERAL
(1649-1651)

After the short Generalate of Vincent Caraffa the 9th General Congregation was called for December 13, 1649. The delegates elected a 75-year old Sienese, Francisco Piccolomini, who had been a teacher of Philosophy and Theology and during his career had been the Provincial of three different provinces—Rome, Milano, and Venice—three more prestigious cities could not have been imagined and his work as Provincial of these three important centers must have taken more time and energy than he could spare.

He was 75 years old when he was elected by 59 votes out of 80 on the 21st of December, a week into the sessions of the 9th Congregation. After only a year and six months as General, Piccolomini died, undoubtedly worn out by the strenuous work required of him as Provincial and then, on top of it all, at his advanced age, they laid upon his shoulders the cares of the whole Society. His death occurred on June 17, 1651. Piccolomini had concerned himself with erecting new provinces, censuring those who would attempt to erect new provinces without authorization, insisting that only men of exceptional virtue should be professed, that the Roman Rite should be observed by all, that useless questions should not be treated in Philosophy or Theology, and that the directions of the General were to be observed.

Some of the external problems of the time were the martyrdoms of the Martyrs of Canada and the upheaval caused by Cromwell and his English Republic.

His remains found their place among those of his predecessors in the crypt of the Gesù.

ALEXANDER GOTTIFREDI S.J. | IX | PRÆP. GEN. | ITAL.

ALEXANDER GOTTIFREDI
NINTH GENERAL
(1652–1652)

Such a short time had passed since the preceding General Congregation, but with Piccolomini's death another had to be called to elect his successor. So, it was called for January 7, 1652 and would last eventually until March 20.

Gottifredi was a Roman by birth, born in 1595 and entered the Society in 1610. He was a well-known preacher in Rome and a teacher of Philosophy and Theology at the Roman College. For a while he was Secretary to Father Vitelleschi and later Roman Provincial. His credentials and lineage were in order for him to be elected by the 10th General Congregation. Two weeks after the Congregation had begun on January 21 Gottifredi was elected General at the age of 57. The Congregation was to have its last session on March 20, but before it could be terminated Gottifredi died on March 12 having been General only two months after a week's illness.

The Senior Assistant immediately took charge. This was Father Banfo the Vicar General, who was to call for another election within a few days.

Gottifredi's remains were placed with those of the previous Generals in the Ossuary in the crypt of the Gesù.

GOSWIN NICKEL S.J. | X | PRÆP. GEN. | GERM.

GOSWIN NICKEL
TENTH GENERAL
(1652–1664)

He was born in Coslar a small town in the Lower Rhine region of Germany on May 1, 1584. He entered the Society on April 3, 1604 and after ordination became professor of Philosophy at Cologne. Then the picture began to emerge as he became first Provincial of Germany and then German Assistant.

The sudden death of Gottifredi caused such consternation that the Delegates of the 10th Congregation were hard put to find a quick successor. They immediately set to work. Another vote was taken in nine days on March 17, 1652 and the delegates elected Father Goswin Nickel a 70-year-old German by 55 votes out of 77. The Congregation was concluded on March 20 on schedule.

During his tenure he was responsible for the founding of missions in the far-flung reaches of the world. He had to encourage and yet moderate his Jesuits in the battle that was raging against Jansenism in France and the Low Countries. After Queen Christina had abdicated her throne in Sweden, had become a Catholic and moved to Rome, she deigned to pay a visit to the Jesuit General.

Because of his infirmities he asked for a Vicar General to assist him and Father John Paul Oliva was appointed to that position on June 7, 1661. Oliva was the right hand of Nickel until at 80 years of age Nickel succumbed to those infirmities and died on July 31, 1664, having been General for twelve years.

His body clothed in priestly vestments was taken to the crypt of the Gesù and placed with those of his predecessors.

JOHN PAUL OLIVA S.J. | XI | PRÆP. GEN. | ITAL.

JOHN PAUL OLIVA
ELEVENTH GENERAL
(1664–1681)

Nine years had passed since the previous General Congregation—the 10th—so, the 11th Congregation was called to last from May 9, 1661 until July 27. The Delegates had a problem. Nickel, who was 80 years old, was seriously incapacitated and had often asked for a Vicar. The Pope was asked to empower the Delegates to designate a Vicar who would have the right of succession and who would immediately be able to act with the full powers of a General. On June 7, 1661 Oliva was chosen as Vicar. Historians Astrain and Bangert both say that Nickel was "General in name only: Oliva in all but name." Nickel lived on in this situation for another three years and finally advanced in age and a very sick man gave up his soul to his Creator. Oliva who had been elected Vicar with the right of succession at the last Congregation, now assumed his complete role as General.

Oliva was a native of Genoa and had entered the Society in 1616. He had been Rector of the German College, Master of Novices, and an outstanding preacher. To his credit, also, and for the benefit of the Society he was on good terms with four Popes.

During the seventeen years and four months of his generalate, Europe was not a peaceful place and Oliva's Jesuits and their works were in constant peril. The Thirty Years War was still being fought; Louis XIV was on the French throne at Versailles for the glory of France and to the misery of the rest of the world. Catholics were persecuted and condemned for a supposed attempt to blow up the Houses of Parliament in London.

But he also had some consoling moments. The Sacred Heart had appeared to a nun in France whose confessor was a Jesuit. The Church of St. Ignatius was finally finished to the admiration of all in 1642. Decoration of the Gesù and the Novitiate Church of St. Andrea al Quirinale was finished to the satisfaction of its architect Bernini, who was a close friend of Oliva.

Oliva died on November 26, 1681 after 17 years and four months as General. His remains were placed in the customary manner in the ossuary reserved for Jesuit Generals in the crypt of the Gesù.

CHARLES DE NOYELLE S.J. | XII | PRÆP. GEN. | BELG.

CHARLES DE NOYELLE
TWELFTH GENERAL
(1682–1686)

He was born in Brussels in Belgium in 1615 and entered the Society at the age of 15 in 1630.

He was 67 years old when, on July 5, he was elected unanimously by the delegates of the 12th General Congregation, which had its opening session on June 22 and was to end on September 6, 1682.

For him his four years and five months as General was sheer agony with Jesuits caught between disagreements and fights between the Bourbons in the person of Louis XIV and the Hapsburgs in the person of Charles II of Spain. Each side would put pressure on de Noyelle and he was mentally crushed trying to placate both these powerful rulers, who had so much influence over Jesuit activities in their countries. De Noyelle tried to tread in midstream fearful of the Jesuits being caught in the undertow. Père de la Chaize, the confessor of Louis XIV, was cold to the demands of the General and ran hot and cold—more French than Jesuit. Eventually, de Noyelle yielded to France, and Spain cut off all communication with the General. Those squabbles between governments and powers and with Jesuits on both sides caused poor de Noyelle no little anxiety and his health began to fail.

Finally, after a generalate of four years and five months he collapsed on December 12, 1686. His death was a merciful release from the pressures he had undergone and he was laid to his eternal rest with his confreres in the crypt of the Gesù.

THYRSUS GONZALEZ S.J. | XIII | PRÆP. GEN. | SPAN.

THYRSUS GONZALEZ
THIRTEENTH GENERAL
(1687-1705)

He was born in 1622 in Argante a small town in Leon, Spain. He had entered the Society at the age of 20 in 1642 and became a renowned parish-mission preacher in a team with a certain Gabriel Guillén. The two of them were known all over Spain for their Parish missions and worked successfully together from 1665 until 1672. Then Gonzalez was appointed to teach Theology at Salamanca and it was there that he became obsessed with the theological opinions known among theologians as probabilism versus probabiliorism, one more rigorous on Moral issues than the other. (I will not go into this esoteric controversy here—it can be found in theological tomes). But, Gonzalez wrote a book defending his position against some of the learned theologians of the Society. The censors refused to permit the book to be published and Gonzalez wrote to Pope Innocent XI asking him to support his book, but Innocent did not want to get into this family squabble

After the death of de Noyelle the 13th General Congregation was called for June 22 until Sept. 7, 1867.

The Pope had made it clear that he wanted the Congregation to elect Gonzalez General and to approve a decree expressly stating that Jesuits were free to defend probabiliorism with a clear conscience. The Congregation voted in that wise. The 65 year old Gonzalez was elected General as Innocent had requested on July 6, 1687.

Nine years later another, the 14th, General Congregation was called by Gonzalez at the request of the Pope. This was done in accord with the decree of Innocent X, which required the Jesuits to have a General Congregation every nine years. So, the 14th Congregation convened in 1696. Everything went well and it ended in peace. In 1702 he sent a memorial to Clement XI complaining that the doctrine of probabilism meant the end of the Society.

Gonzalez was 80 years old by this time and was failing physically. His Assistants advised him to choose a Vicar General and he chose Michelangelo Tamburini to help him. The next "9 year" General Congregation was coming closer and was called for January 1706. The General insisted on imposing his own moral ideas on the whole Society and the Theologians balked. As the delegates began arriving in Rome for the 15th General Congregation, Thyrsus Gonzalez was called to his eternal reward and a great sigh of relief was heard among the delegates and in Jesuit houses around the world. God had solved a vexing internal problem. After a Generalate of 18 years and 3 months Gonzalez died on October 27, 1705 and was laid to rest with the remains of the previous Fathers General in the crypt of the Gesù.

MICHAEL ANGELO TAMBURINI S.J. | XIV | PRÆP. GEN. | ITAL

MICHAEL ANGELO TAMBURINI
FOURTEENTH GENERAL
(1706–1730)

H e was born in Modena on September 27, 1648. He had entered the Society at the age of 17 after attending the local Jesuit College. After his course of studies, of which he was an apt pupil, he taught Scholastic Philosophy at Bologna and Theology at Mantua for the next twelve years. Successively he became rector of various colleges, then, the Provincial of the Venetian Province, Secretary to the General and, finally, due to Gonzalez' feebleness, he became Vicar General. Since before his death Gonzalez had called for the 15th General Congregation, the fathers decided to go ahead with it.

The delegates convened on January 20, 1706 and on the 31st of that month elected Michael Angelo Tamburini, the 58-year-old Italian from Modena as the 14th General.

Though the foreign missions were a prime concern of almost every General, Tamburini went at it with vigor. During his generalate the famous Paraguay Reductions were encouraged and promoted. He established missions in the Near East and in the Far East he gave his approval to the "de Nobili" experiment in India. These seeming innovations did not set well with the commercial interests of the great European investments. There was an undercurrent of opposition against the Jesuits which would eventually lead to the Suppression of the Society within the next half-century.

The Jansenists, too, piqued by their reversals engineered by the Jesuits were in the first row accusing the Jesuits of various nefarious schemes. The missions, especially, were accused of drawing mission lands away from the Church and away from the influence of Portugal, Spain, and France. Tamburini, however, made a special visit to the Pope to assure him of the Society's complete compliance with his directives and steadfast loyalty to the Church.

During the 24 years and one month of his Generalate, Tamburini was the constant target of slander and calumny and frequently lampooned and caricatured viciously in tracts published by the enemies of the Society. They sought to insult him with cynical cartoons in every attack. Jesuits were accused of betraying the Church in mission countries. But worst of all were the factions that split the Society, itself, and certainly weakened it for the blow which was to come. Attacked from all sides and worn out by confusion and accusation that he was not keeping his Jesuits in order and having submitted to the burden for 24 years he died at the age of 82 on February 28, 1730. After his funeral in the Gesù his remains were carried to the crypt and laid to rest.

Francis Retz S.J. | XV | Præp. Gen. | Bohem.

FRANCIS RETZ
FIFTEENTH GENERAL
(1730–1750)

F rancis Retz was born in Prague, Bohemia in 1673 and entered the Society at the age of 16 in 1689. He became a professor of Philosophy at Olmutz on the Danube and later became a professor of Theology at the Clementinum in Prague where he was also appointed Rector. Later he became Provincial of Bohemia and in 1725 the German Assistant.

Before Tamburini had died he had failed to appoint a Vicar General, so the Professed Fathers assembled and elected Retz Vicar General on the first ballot.

He then called a General Congregation—the 16th—for November 19, 1730. The 57-year-old Retz was elected General unanimously, except for his own vote on November 30.

The Catholic Church and especially the Jesuits was on the defensive all over Europe and in the missions it was almost the same. The Jesuits did not seem to have any champion to lead a counter-attack. Despite the vicissitudes the Society continued to grow to over 22,000 members and 39 Provinces. By some individuals, great strides were being made, but aside from occasional cries of success, nothing of great importance was being accomplished.

Retz was General for 20 years and died on November 19, 1750. Only a few short years later the Man-of-War he captained was sunk.

The last remains of Retz were carried to the crypt of the Gesù where they would peacefully rest with his predecessors.

IGNATIUS VISCONTI S.J. | XVI | PRÆP. GEN. | ITAL.

IGNATIUS VISCONTI
SIXTEENTH GENERAL
(1751-1755)

The tenure of this General was among the shortest of all the Generals. He was in office for only three years and ten months. He was originally from Milano, had been professor of Rhetoric, Philosophy, Theology, and Superior of the Jesuit Church of San Fedele in Milano, a few paces from the famous cathedral. Then, he became Provincial, Assistant and Vicar General. When Retz died after his twenty years in office, the delegates to the 17th General Congregation elected the 69 year old Visconti on July 4, 1751 a couple of weeks after the Congregation had begun. It lasted from its opening on June 22 until September 5, 1751.

During his generalate, short as it was, he was able to get off some letters to the whole Society on the use of Studies and the value of Poverty, but he really had little time to accomplish much. His letter to the Austrian Jesuits was on the value of the use of Latin or, in some cases, use of the vernacular. The Jesuit response to these letters was less than encouraging as was the Jesuit weak or non-existent response to the government's programs for the colleges. The Reductions in Paraguay were forced to re-locate, but the import of these hedgings did not seem to be understood and the Society became more divided and weak, seemingly waiting for the end, which many could see coming. His short term ended when he died on May 4, 1755.

After the usual service in the Gesù his remains were carried to the crypt.

ALOYSIUS CENTURIONE S.J. | XVII | PRÆP. GEN. | ITAL.

ALOYSIUS CENTURIONE
SEVENTEENTH GENERAL
(1755-1757)

He was born in Genoa in 1686 and entered the Society when he was 17 years old in 1703. After receiving his Liberal Arts Degree he taught Philosophy and Theology. In 1751 he became Assistant for Italy and, then, Vicar General to Father Visconti.

After the death of Visconti, Centurione summoned a General Congregation for November 18, 1735, and twelve days later on November 30 he was elected General. He was elected on the second ballot. It was Sunday, the Feast of St. Andrew and he was 69 years old.

Father Centurione's term as General was one of the shortest on record, since it was brought to a quick conclusion by his death after only a year and ten months in office. He had not much more time than to write one letter to the Society on the spirit of our vocations and to demote the house in Tusculum (Tivoli) to a residence subject to Rome.

He died at the age of 71 on October 2, 1757, and his remains were carefully placed in the crypt of the Gesù beside those of his predecessors.

Lorenzo Ricci S.J. | XVIII | Præp. Gen. | Ital.

LORENZO RICCI
EIGHTEENTH GENERAL
(1758-1775)

At the unforeseen death of Father Centurione after less than two years, Father Giovanni Antonio Timoni, the Vicar General, called for a General Congregation—the nineteenth—to begin on May 9, 1758. On May 21—Trinity Sunday—the election was held and the Fathers elected 55-year-old Lorenzo Ricci, the Secretary of the Society, as General. He was elected by over half the votes on the second ballot.

Ricci had been born in Florence in 1703 and had entered the Society fifteen years later. He had taught Rhetoric, Philosophy, and Theology in Siena for six years, was Secretary of the Society for two years, and the revered Spiritual Director of the students at the Roman College.

Those were very trying years for the Society and for the General to see it heading towards dissolution. All the governments of Europe had been ranged against it for several years and during preceding generalates. Ricci had to face the culmination of what had been prepared for years and partly, perhaps, at the fault of the Society itself. Pope Clement XIV was, finally, blackmailed to issue the letter of Suppression for which he is unjustly condemned by some. The Society was forbidden to receive Novices and the houses of the Society were confiscated and the Churches given to others. The whole world seemed to be in upheaval. George III of England was having his problems with his unruly colony on the other side of the Atlantic. Louis XV had died in France and left the country in the hands of a son—sincere but incapable —to rule as did his predecessors. In Portugal a 72-year-old Jesuit, who had been a missionary in Brazil, was accused of being an accomplice in a plot to kill the king. He was imprisoned in the Belem Tower. His imprisonment reduced him to seeing bizarre visions. The poor old man was finally found guilty of heresy, condemned by the Inquisition, dragged from prison to the Rossio Square in Lisbon, there strangled, and his body burned at the stake in the presence of the king.

All countries were expelling the Jesuits and shipping them by whatever means to the Papal States. Some, too old for such treatment died and others left Religion or became secular priests. By 1773 the Suppression was complete. On August 16 the Brief of Suppression was read to the assembled Jesuits and they dispersed to various locales and to other works. On August 17 Ricci, the unfortunate General, was bundled off to prison in Castel Sant'Angelo where he languished for two years not even permitted to celebrate Mass or receive visitors. Eventually he died there on November 24, 1775 after 15 years as General. He testified to the end that the Society was innocent of all the accusations thrown against it.

By order of Pope Pius VI his solemn funeral was held in the Church of San Giovanni de' Fiorentini the church closest to Ricci's prison. By order of the same Pope his body was taken to the Gesù a few hundred meters away and laid to rest in the crypt with the Generals who preceded him.

However, Ricci's imprisonment and death and the Letter of Suppression did not bring the desired end of the Society.

The Letter was valid only in those countries where it was officially promulgated. Frederick of Prussia recognizing the value of the Jesuits as educators refused to promulgate the Brief. So, too, Catherine II of Russia forbade its promulgation for the same reason, recognizing that without the education provided by the Jesuits there would be disastrous effects on her subjects. At first, some Jesuits became parish priests and continued to teach in the Jesuit Colleges as before.

Since they were recognized legally as Jesuits in those two countries, the Fathers in White Russia called a General Congregation—The First in White Russia. They elected as Vicar General the 53-year-old Father Stanislaus Czerniewicz. He was a leading Jesuit of the Province and was Rector at the College at Polotsk.

With both Papal acquiescence and Royal approval the Jesuits continued to live and work as Jesuits. Catherine encouraged them to open a Novitiate and paid no heed to other governments who opposed what she did in her own realm.

Stanislaus Czerniewicz died on July 7, 1785 and the Fathers called the Second Congregation of White Russia to elect a successor. They elected as Vicar General Father Gabriel Lenkiewicz on September 27. He held the office until he died on November 10, 1798. The Third Congregation in White Russia was held early in 1799 and on February 1 Father Franz Xaver Kareu was elected Vicar General. But, in a Papal brief dated 1801 it was permitted that the General Superior would no longer be designated as Vicar General, but with the title of General as was held before the Suppression. Kareu died on July 30, 1802.

By 1800 there were over 200 Jesuits in Russia and many others scattered about Europe—officially linked to the Jesuits who were subjects of the Tsar.

After Father Kareu's death the 4th General Congregation in Russia was held in Poland and on October 10 the delegates elected Father Gabriel Gruber as General of the now fully vital Society. On March 26,

1805 his residence caught fire and Father Gruber was burned to death. The Congregation designated as the Fifth in White Russia was held in Poland and on September 2 elected Thaddeus Brzozowski, a 65-year-old Pole, as General.

Subsequently, the Society was restored to the world by the Papal letter "Solicitudine Omnium Ecclesiarum" on August 14, 1814. What had been lost had been found. The Society was reborn.

STANISLAUS CZERNIEWICZ S.J. | VIC. GEN. | POLON.

GABRIEL LEINKIEWICZ S.J. | VIC. GEN. | POLON.

FRANZ XAVER KAREU S.J. | VIC. GEN. | POLON.

GABRIEL GRUBER S.J. | VIC. GEN. | AUSTR.

THADDEUS BRZOZOWSKI S.J. | XIX | PRÆP. GEN. | POLON.

THADDEUS BRZOZOWSKI
NINETEENTH GENERAL
(1805–1820)

He was elected general in Poland on September 2, 1805. In 1814 when the Society was restored to the whole world a new election was unnecessary and Father Brzozowski retained the title and the office for the whole Society. He was the link which bound the two parts of the Society together.

He had been born in Poland on October 21, 1749 and entered the Society in Russia on February 2, 1784. He was a successful and well-known preacher and was named Vicar General by Father Kareu in 1797. He died at the age of 71 and was buried in his native Poland.

LUIGI FORTIS S.J. | XX | PRÆP. GEN. | ITAL.

LUIGI FORTIS
TWENTIETH GENERAL
(1820-1829)

He was born on February 26, 1748 in Verona, Italy, and had been admitted to the Venice Province on October 12, 1762, at the tender age of 14. He taught the Humanities in Ferrara. When the Society was suppressed he went to Parma at the request of the Duke and became Director of the College of Nobles. He re-entered the Society in 1794 and became Provincial for Italy. After the death of Brzozowski the General Congregation was held between October 9, 1820 and December 10, 1820.

On October 18 Father Fortis was elected General at the age of 72. During his generalate he vigorously promoted the formation of Novices and Scholastics. He saw the return to the Society of the Roman College, of the German College, and of the College of Nobles. From Pope Leo XII Father Fortis obtained confirmation of many of the former privileges enjoyed by the Society. He saw, also, the return of Jesuit houses from Piedmont to Sardinia.

After being General for eight years and three months he died in Rome on January 27, 1829. He was buried in the crypt of the Gesù.

JOANNES ROOTHAAN S.J. | XXI | PRÆP. GEN. | OLAND.

JOANNES ROOTHAAN
TWENTY-FIRST GENERAL
(1829-1853)

He was born in Amsterdam on November 23, 1785 of parents who had emigrated from Frankfurt, and who had also converted from Calvinism. Under the apt guidance of a former Jesuit, who had been caught in the Suppression, and of another under whom he studied the classics he went to Dvinck (Duneburg) in White Russia so he could enter the Society, which he did, on June 18, 1804.

In Poland as a scholastic he taught Classics and Rhetoric and was ordained in 1812 at Polotsk. On August 14, 1814 when Pope Pius VII restored the Society, Roothaan was in Pusza. When the Jesuits were expelled from Russia by the Tsar, Roothaan fled to the Jesuit College at Brig in Switzerland where he taught Rhetoric and preached parish missions in the whole Vallesia region along the upper reaches of the Inn River. He founded the College at Turin and became its Rector.

The Congregation held after the death of Father Fortis was held between June 20, 1829 and August 17. On July 9 Roothaan, only 44 years old, was elected General, the youngest since Acquaviva.

During his generalate the secular world, too, was changing. Napoleon had been defeated and exiled; the Catholic Hierarchy was restored in England. Belgium became an independent country and Victoria had begun her long reign as Queen/Empress. Roothaan saw his Jesuits expelled from several countries only to expand to newer corners of the Lord's vineyard. The Belgian, DeSmet, went to evangelize the American Indians in the Rocky Mountains and the Far West. Jesuits expelled from Italy founded colleges and missions. The influential Italian review, Civiltà Cattolica, was founded in Naples in 1850, later to move to Rome. So, despite the many heartaches Roothaan suffered, as his Jesuits suffered, he also received many consolations. He bore the burden for 23 years and 10 months and died at age 68 on May 8, 1853. His remains lie beneath an altar in the Gesù and his heart is kept in a reliquary at the Jesuit Curia in Rome.

PETER JOANNES BECKX S.J. | XXII | PRÆP. GEN. | BELG.

PETER JOANNES BECKX
TWENTY-SECOND GENERAL
(1853-1887)

Peter was a Belgian born on February 8, 1795 in Sichem near Diest in the Diocese of Mechlin. He was 20 years old when he entered the seminary at Mechlin, but eight months after his ordination he decided to become a Jesuit. On October 29, 1819, at the age of 24, he entered the Society at Hildesheim. He became the chaplain and confessor of Duke Ferdinand d'Anhalt-Koethen and after the death of the Duke he rendered the same service for the Duchess when she moved to Vienna. In 1850 he became Rector of Louvain and professor of Canon Law. Then, two years later, he became the Provincial of Austria.

After Roothaan's death, the 22nd General Congregation was called to be in session from June 22 to last until August 31, 1853. On July 2 this Congregation elected the 58-year-old Beckx as General.

European politics at that time were in a sorry state and governments shifted from monarchy to republic overnight. It was a time of political unrest and there seemed to be a revolution going on somewhere at any given time. In Italy, too, the reunification was taking place with no one really knowing what it meant or how it would be accomplished.

At the establishment of the Republic in 1873 the Jesuits were expelled from the Collegio Romano losing title to the name as well as to the property. They moved into the German College on via del Seminario, changed its name to Università Gregoriana del Collegio Romano, and remained in that location until the political situation had changed in 1930 when they moved into their new building near the Quirinale.

In 1873, too, it was judged prudent to move the Curia. On October 30, 1873 the General and two Fathers moved to the Villa San Girolomo in Fiesole, which, then, became the seat of the Jesuit Curia Generalis. The air was certainly better there than in Rome both physically and politically.

On May 11, 1883 Father Beckx announced that he was convening the 23rd General Congregation for September 15. The reason for this announcement was that, with the Holy Father's consent, he had selected Father Antonio Maria Anderledy as his permanent Vicar General with the right of succession. He wanted the approval of the General Congregation for this decision. Beckx was getting feeble and needed the help of a trusted lieutenant. The Fathers of the Congregation approved his plan of action after Leo XIII asked Beckx to remain and give guidance. On September 24, 1883, Beckx then imposed silence on the whole Congregation in reference to this affair.

On January 20, 1884 Beckx gave up almost all his authority as General into the hands of Anderledy. He then retired to the German College in Rome where he lingered on quite feeble and finally died three years later on March 4, 1887. Anderledy then succeeded him as the 23rd General.

Beckx had been General for 33 years and 8 months, from 1853 until 1887, when he died at age 88 years in Rome.

During his generalate literary progress had been made by the founding of the now famous Jesuit journals, *La Civiltà Cattolica* in Naples then moving to Rome, *Razon y Fe* in Madrid, and the first issue of *Etudes* came out in Paris. The body of Father Peter Beckx was taken to the Campo Verano Cemetery of Rome where it was interred in the newly constructed Jesuit Mausoleum.

ANTONIO MARIA ANDERLEDY S.J. | XXIII | PRÆP. GEN. | HEL

ANTONIO MARIA ANDERLEDY
TWENTY-THIRD GENERAL
(1887-1892)

He was born in the small town of Berisal in Switzerland not far from the northern border of Italy in the Vallais region where the Inn River is still a rushing mountain stream. He was a student at the Jesuit College in Brig. It would not be too far fetched to surmise that Anderledy, as a boy, had heard the successful preaching of Jan Roothaan, who worked up and down that same valley and from that contact, perhaps, received the grace of his vocation.

So, Anderledy entered the Society on October 5, 1858 and because of delicate health and political reasons was sent to the Jesuit Theologate in the Missouri Province of the U.S. After ordination he was then sent to work for a time among the American Indians at Green Bay, Wisconsin, where the Jesuits had established a mission.

After a short time he returned to Germany and became an outstanding preacher of the popular parish missions as Roothaan had done in Anderledy's native valley in Switzerland. Successively, he became Rector, Provincial and, finally, German Assistant in 1870. In 1883 he was appointed by Father Beckx as his Vicar General with the right of succession. With the death of Beckx, Anderledy took over the governance of the Society. He was 64 years old when he succeeded Beckx and was General for only four years and ten months from the death of Beckx until his own death on January 18, 1892.

During his generalate he promoted by letter solid formation of his subjects, the teaching of St. Thomas and gave impulse to literary and scientific efforts. As a close personal friend of Leo XIII he was able to obtain for the Society more of the former privileges the Society had lost during the suppression. Though his health was not strong, he accomplished much in a short time by his strong will.

His death occurred at Fiesole and he was interred in the church of Villa San Girolamo, because the Fathers were afraid that a public display at Anderledy's funeral, if it were held in Rome, would cause too much disturbance.

Years later the Jesuit Provincial of the Florence area decided to have one tomb for all the Jesuits who had died in the Florence Province. A burial plot was purchased in the Florence Municipal Cemetery and the bones of the Jesuits were brought together. Anderledy's remains are there, listed with all the others, with the sole distinction of "Praep. Gen." following his name.

LUIS MARTIN S.J. | XXIV | PRÆP. GEN. | SPAN.

LUIS MARTIN
TWENTY-FOURTH GENERAL
(1892-1906)

L uis was born on August 19, 1846 the third of the seven children of Clemente and Francisca Garcia of Melgar in Castile, Spain. He entered the Society on October 13, 1864 at the age of 18 and made his Novitiate at Loyola in Spain. He studied Philosophy at Vals in France and was ordained on September 24, 1876 by Bishop Juan Camillo Fonteneau, Bishop of Agen, France. He celebrated his first Mass at the shrine of Lourdes, which, at that time, was just beginning its fame. He became a Rector, then, Provincial of Castile and Sub-Secretary of the Society. After Anderledy's death the political situation was so tense that Pope Leo XIII suggested that the General Congregation, that was to be called, should take place some-where outside Italy. The Vicar General deemed it appropriate that it should be held at Loyola, Spain.

So, the 24th General Congregation was held in Spain from September 24 until December 5, 1892. The Vicar General, Luis Martin, was elected General on October 2, 1892 at the age of 48. The Congregation also recommended that the General and Curia should return to Rome from Fiesole. In January 1895 this was done and the Curia took up its residence in the German College. Beckx had left Rome 22 years before, but by now the political and religious climate had changed sufficiently to warrant a return.

Martin was a man of great ideas and one of his most outstanding was the writing of the definitive history of the Society from its Ignatian beginnings using all available documents. This project became the famous *Monumenta Historica*, which at this writing is made up of over 150 thick volumes, written by Jesuits competent in their specific fields. He also encouraged Jesuits of other countries to write the histories of their provinces, which was done at times with such vigor that these Histories now take up much space on the shelves of Jesuit house libraries.

In 1905 cancer was discovered on his right arm. The arm had to be amputated after several attempts, of finding a cure, were unsuccessful.

Eventually, he died on April 18, 1906 at the age of 60 years, and a generalate of 13 years and 6 months. He was interred in the large Jesuit Mausoleum in the Roman cemetery at Campo Verano.

FRANZ XAVER WERNZ S.J. | XXV | PRÆP. GEN. | GERM.

FRANZ XAVER WERNZ
TWENTY-FIFTH GENERAL
(1906–1914)

Father Wernz was born on December 4, 1842 in Rotweil, Wurtemburg in Germany on the edge of the Black Forest. He was the first of the eight children of parents with deep faith and piety. From an early age he had expressed his desire to be a Jesuit, perhaps influenced by the fact that his parish church in Rottweil had been a Jesuit church before the suppression and still retained many reminders of the Society. The paintings of so many Jesuit Saints and the fact that the yearly parish mission was given by Jesuits probably helped him to make that important decision. He entered the Society on December 5, 1857, made his Novitiate at Gorheim near Sigmaringen, and took his first Vows on December 8, 1859. His Philosophy studies were made at Aachen and Maria Laach and when the Kulturkampf of Chancellor Bismarck expelled the Jesuits from Germany, the exiled scholastics found refuge in the Jesuit College, Ditton Hall in Lancastershire in England and, finally, in 1881 moved to St. Bueno's in Wales. After a year of private study he became Professor of Canon Law at Ditton Hall and later at St. Bueno's in Wales. Between 1882 and 1906 he taught Canon Law at the Gregorian University on via del Seminario, the last two years spent there he also served as its Rector. He was a renowned Canonist and was much sought after by various Vatican Congregations on which he served with devotion and conscientiousness.

After the death of Father Martin, the Vicar General summoned a Congregation for August 31, 1906, but it began after a day's postponement on September 1 and would last until October 18. On the third ballot taken on September 8, the 64-year-old Wernz was elected General.

During his generalate he vigorously promoted the spiritual life, opened missions and created provinces in all parts of the world. The whole continent of North America was one of his special interests and he approved the setting up of provinces, houses, and colleges the length and breadth of that vast territory. Martin had set up the famous *Monumenta Historica* and Wernz continued his support and encouraged Jesuit writers to take up this important work, which they did with enthusiasm. He was instrumental in the founding of the Jesuit periodicals "Voces e Maria ad Lacum" which became "Stimmen der Zeit" in Germany and another, "Przeglad Powszechny," in Poland.

One of his last letters written on December 25, 1913 to the Society was on the celebration of the centenary of the Society's restitution, to take place the following year.

Wernz had been General for seven years and eleven months, from September 8, 1906 until he died on August 19, 1914. His death occurred only a few hours before that of the saintly Pontiff Pope Pius X and a mere three weeks after the outbreak of the First World War. It would be a difficult time for his successor to begin leading an international Society in a world internationally shattered.

His tomb can be found in the Jesuit Mausoleum at the Roman Campo Verano cemetery.

WLODIMIR LEDOCHOWSKI S.J. | XXVI | PRÆP. GEN. | POLON

WLODIMIR LEDOCHOWSKI
TWENTY-SIXTH GENERAL
(1915–1942)

He was born the only son of Count Antonius Kalka Ledochowski on the family estate a few miles north of Vienna in Loosdorf. Though of Polish ancestry, the land—at that time in history—was under Hapsburg rule, so the family was nominally Austrian.

In a family where two sisters had preceded him, the birth of a son on October 7, 1866 was a cause for rejoicing.

He studied at the Jesuit Secondary School, the Theresianum, in Vienna and for a time was page to the Empress. He studied Law at the University of Crakow and then began studies for the secular priesthood. At the age of 23, while attending the Gregorian University on via Del Seminario in Rome, he decided to become a Jesuit and entered the Society in 1889. Five years later he was ordained a Jesuit priest. At first he took to writing, but was soon made Superior of the Jesuit residence in Cracow, then, Rector of the College. He became the Polish Vice-Provincial in 1901 and Provincial of Galicia in 1902. From 1906 until February 1915 he was the German Assistant.

After the death of Wernz the 26th General Congregation was convened which would last from February 2, 1915 until March 18 and be held in the Germanico-Hungarico College. The 49-year-old Wlodimir Ledochowski was elected the 26th General of the Society on February 11 on the second ballot.

Despite the upheaval of the World War and the economic Depression of the 1930s, the Society increased during Ledochowski's term in office.

He called the 27th General Congregation to take place at the Germanico to acquaint the Society with the new code of Canon Law and to bring the Jesuit Constitutions into line with it. He called another Congregation (the 28th)—between March 12 and May 9, 1937—in order for the delegates to appoint a Vicar General as he was now feeling the effects of age and needed competent assistance. He established the Oriental Institute and the Russian College as well as the Institutum Biblicum of the Gregorian University. He saw a certain emancipation of the Society after the Concordat between the Church and the Italian Government was ratified. Property was returned to the Society making it possible for the Jesuits to build a new Gregorian University building transferring from the Palazzo Borgomeo on via del Seminario to Piazza Pilotta within a few paces of the Quirinal Palace. He then built the new Curia Generalis on property acquired from the Vatican on Borgo Santo Spirito—about a hundred meters from St. Peter's Square. The Concordat, somewhat engineered by a Jesuit, Father Tacchi-Venturi, put new life into the Society and its property increased with its influence and reputation.

Ledochowski's Generalate was one of the most productive, physically as well as spiritually, certainly since the restoration. Ledochowski also saw the beginnings of the Second World War and was torn by the sufferings of his Jesuit sons on both sides.

After 27 years and 10 months as General—from February 11, 1915 until December 13, 1942—he devoutly rendered his soul to God and, after his funeral in the Gesù his remains were taken to the Society's mausoleum at Campo Verano on the eastern edge of Rome, where they were interred.

JOHN-BAPTIST JANSSENS S.J. | XXVII | PRÆP. GEN. | BELG.

JOHN-BAPTIST JANSSENS
TWENTY-SEVENTH GENERAL
(1946–1964)

He was born in Mechelen, Belgium three days before Christmas on December 22, 1889. His first schooling was in the Diocesan Secondary School in Hasselt and his university years, where he excelled in Philosophy and Classical Philology, were spent at St. Aloysius University Faculty in Brussels. He entered the Jesuit Novitiate in Drongen on September 23, 1907, and took his first Vows in September 1909.

After the usual two years of Philosophy spent at the Jesuit Collegium Maximum in Leuven he won his Doctorate in Civil Law at the University of Louvain (Leuven).

From 1921 to 1923 he attended the Gregorian University in Rome where he added a Doctorate in Canon Law to the one he had earned at Louvain.

He taught Canon Law at the Collegium Maximum in Louvain from 1923 until 1929 and became its Rector on August 17, 1929. On August 15, 1935 he was appointed Tertian Master and in 1938 became Provincial of the Northern Belgian Province of the Jesuits.

During the year 1939 in the name of the General he made an official visit to the Jesuit missions in Zaire, at the time a protectorate of Belgium and known as the Belgian Congo. With the exception of this visitation and his two years studying in Rome, he had spent most of his life in his own province—in Leuven, Drongen, Antwerp, and Brussels.

When Father Ledochowski died in 1942 the war was in full fury in Europe and Father Janssens was the Jesuit Provincial trying to keep his province intact and in peace. The Vicar General, Norbert de Boyne was unable to call a General Congregation because of the war. Thus, in effect, de Boyne was in charge of the governance of the Society for three years.

The war ended in August 1945 and de Boyne was finally able to convene a General Congregation—the 29th—between September 6 and October 23, 1946. Janssens, as Provincial of his province, went to Rome as a delegate. The Congregation was held under Spartan conditions and many of the necessaries were provided by the delegates themselves from countries less affected by the war than were the countries of Europe.

On September 15, Father Janssens the 57-year old Belgian was elected General on the first ballot and became the first General in the Nuclear Age.

Because of his delicate health and the oppressiveness of the Roman air, a sizeable piece of property in the Alban Hills—southeast of Rome —was purchased as a retreat for the general and his curia. This property, well known in the area as Villa Cavalletti, became a place of retreat not only for the General and the Curia but also for the other Jesuits of Rome. It was also used and appreciated by professors and students of the Gregorian University—who could manage to get away for a few days of peace. It was finally sold in 1995, long after Father Janssens was in his grave.

In 1957 after eleven years in office he summoned the 30th General Congregation to provide him with a Vicar General. During its September 6 to November 11 session the delegates appointed Father John Swain, a Canadian, as his Vicar.

In his final years Janssens had to confront a dissension which was arising among theologians inside and outside the Society. He tried to moderate the problem, but to no avail, since the difficulty was not only within the Society, but also throughout the whole Church. He was the last to see the numbers in the Society top out at 36,000 members. After which high point there was a steady drop for the next thirty years. The turmoil in the Society and in the Church would not go away.

Pope John XXIII had convened Vatican Council II to begin in 1962 to deal with many of the same problems that plagued Janssens during his generalate, and with which he found it difficult to cope.

After 18 years and one month as General, Father Janssens died at the age of 75 on October 5, 1964. His body was taken to the Jesuit mausoleum at Campo Verano and interred with his immediate predecessors.

PERDO ARRUPE S.J. | XXVIII | PRÆP. GEN. | SPAN.

PEDRO ARRUPE
TWENTY-EIGHTH GENERAL
(1965–1983)

For anyone familiar with the Jesuits and living in the last quarter of the 20th Century, the name Pedro Arrupe, the 28th General of the Society of Jesus, needs no introduction.

No man, Pope or saint, you or I, is without advocates and opponents. In some cases there are more and in others, less, some are of little or no value and others may be more discerning. Arrupe, too, has had these; not only in his lifetime, but also since the day he passed into history. When discussing the possibility of Arrupe's beatification, one Jesuit remarked that it probably would not happen until all his enemies were dead. So, our little sketch here will have to look forward to some time in the future when the final word of Arrupe's life is written.

For our purpose, then, we will have to aim at some of the peaks of his life.

He was born on November 14, 1907 into a well-to-do Basque family in Bilbao, Spain, his father being a well-known journalist of that city. In the family he was preceded by four sisters, who, not strangely, took to being doting surrogate mothers. He was baptized on the following day in the fine gothic Cathedral of St. James.

In his early years he was schooled by the Piarist Fathers of Bilbao. While he was at Medical school in Valladolid, his encounter with the Jesuits occurred when he joined the Sodality of Our Lady and St. Stanislaus Kostka, in which he eventually became Prefect and editor of their modest publication. In this he displayed a journalistic bent inherited from his father, one of the founders of the "Gaceta del Norte," a leading journal of Bilbao.

During the 20s there was much social unrest in Spain and a coup d'etat was forced on the king, Alfonso XIII. In 1923 the dictatorship of Primo de Rivera took over the government. In 1930 the king was forced into exile and the anti-Catholic Republican regime took charge. Eventually, General Francisco Franco organized opposition to the government and the Civil War would begin in 1933 and would last until 1936.

Pedro entered the Society on January 15, 1927 at Loyola, the birthplace of St. Ignatius. It is understandable that a Novitiate under such political turmoil would be less than ideal and superiors finally decided to send the scholastics out of the country for their subsequent formation. So, Arrupe was sent with the other scholastics to Marneffe in Belgium and to Valkenburg in Holland. The Jesuits were ultimately expelled from Spain, and some who stayed behind became martyrs during the ensuing civil war.

As an example of those troubled times, the Jesuit church in Madrid had been attacked by a mob and burned to the ground. This action left the Society with only a handful of ashes—which was all that remained—of the bodies of Lainez and Borgia, previous Generals, who had been interred in the church.

On July 30, 1936 Arrupe was ordained a priest at Marneffe, Belgium. That same year he was permitted to participate in the International Conference on Eugenics for those specializing in medicine and psychiatry.

Superiors then sent him to St. Mary's College, the Jesuit Theologate in Kansas, to finish his Theology. His Tertianship, the year terminating his spiritual formation, was spent in Cleveland, Ohio, where he occupied himself with the spiritual direction and care of Hispanic immigrants.

After Tertianship he was sent to the Japanese Mission, where he familiarized himself with the Japanese working for the social services sponsored by Sophia University, the Jesuit university in Tokyo, and in 1940, he spent 35 days as a prisoner of war, accused of spying.

In 1945 he was appointed Jesuit Superior, as well as Novice Master and Rector of the Novitiate and Scholasticate in a suburb of Hiroshima, about three miles from the city center.

On August 6 of that year the Atomic Age was brutally ushered in by the devastating destruction caused by the first Atom Bomb, which destroyed the center of Hiroshima.

With his medical background he was able to organize an emergency hospital, at the Novitiate, to take care of the many casualties fleeing from the center of the city and to alleviate the suffering of hundreds of bewildered and half-dying victims.

After the unimaginable destruction caused by the atomic bomb the war was soon concluded in August 1945. In March 1954 he was named Vice-Provincial and in October 1958 Provincial of the Jesuits in Japan. The call went out world wide for Jesuits to help in the reconstruction of Japan and Jesuits from over 30 countries eagerly and generously responded.

After the death of Janssens in October of 1964, the 31st General Congregation was called to convene in two sessions: the first from May 7 to July 15, 1965 and the second from September 8 to November 17, 1966. Pedro Arrupe was elected General on May 22, 1965 during the first session.

Nine years later at the urging of his collaborators in the Curia, he called the 32nd General Congregation—to face up to and deal with the reaction and response of the Society to the changes occurring in the modern secular world. It lasted from December 2, 1974 to March 7, 1975.

During his tenure he was able to visit Jesuits and their works in all parts of the world. On August 7, 1981 after a long and tiring trip throughout the Far East he suffered a stroke just after his airplane had landed at Rome's Fiumicino Airport. He was paralyzed on his right side and was able to speak only a few words, but this ability gradually deteriorated until he was completely mute. From that time on he lived in the infirmary at the Curia. His only form of communication with the Jesuit Brother, his constant companion, was with his eyes or hand pressure.

The 33rd General Congregation was called to deal with the situation, viz, the resignation of Arrupe and the election of a successor. The Congregation was called by Father Paolo Dezza, the Pontifical Delegate, especially appointed by the Pope to assure that the Society be kept on course. There was a wave of resentment from some Jesuits at what was seemingly Papal interference in Jesuit affairs. However, reading these brief accounts of previous Generals, one might understand that it was quite a normal thing to do; and, the Pope was often unjustly maligned mostly through ignorance of the history of the Society.

Arrupe's resignation was accepted on September 3, 1983 during the Congregation and it proceeded to elect Father Peter-Hans Kolvenbach as General.

During his ten long and silent years in the infirmary, praying for the Society, Arrupe received many and frequent well wishers among whom the Pope was the most distinguished.

He finally died at the Curia on February 5, 1991 in his 84th year. His Generalate actually lasted for 18 years from his election until his resignation in 1983, though he lived another eight years of complete inactivity paralyzed and with little communication.

Pedro Arrupe's funeral was held in the Gesù and was attended by crowds inside and in the piazza outside the church. Also in attendance were 10 cardinals, 20 bishops, the Prime Minister of Italy and other religious and civil dignitaries. His body was taken and interred in the Jesuit Mausoleum at Campo Verano beside his predecessors.

PETER-HANS KOLVENBACH S.J. | XXIX | PRÆP. GEN. | OLANI

PETER-HANS KOLVENBACH
TWENTY-NINTH GENERAL
(1983–PRESENT)

As was written in the previous sketch, any person of the last quarter of the 20th Century, and one familiar with the very recent history of the Jesuits, recognizes the name of Peter-Hans Kolvenbach, the 29th General of the Society. We must await the definitive account of his Generalate to give us a true picture of his accomplishments and hopes for the future of the Society and how they were carried out.

Peter-Hans was born on November 30, 1928, in Druten, a small town in South-eastern Holland, not far from Nijmegen. He was fortunate to have spent his childhood and adolescence close to the German border where he was able not only to use his native Dutch language, but German as well. It gave him a certain linguistic bent and later he was able to acquire several other languages including Arabic and Chaldean. He was able to switch rather easily from one to another without missing a syllable.

His early schooling was at Canisius College, and he soon felt the call to become a priest. He entered the Novitiate at Mariendaal on September 7, 1948 and studied Philosophy and Theology in Nijmegen. He was ordained in Beyrout, Lebanon, on June 29, 1961 in the Chaldean Rite.

He became professor of Linguistics and Armenian at St. Joseph's University and was at home in both Oriental and Occidental communities.

He was named Vice Provincial of the Near East Vice-Province made up of three Regions—Egypt, Lebanon, and Syria. During his term as Vice-Provincial, Lebanon was engaged in a destructive and bloody civil war and Kolvenbach managed to keep his equilibrium, his altruism, and personal tranquility in the face of opposing factions.

He was able to travel through the Near-East visiting the Jesuits in his charge.

In 1981, he was appointed Rector at the Oriental Institute in Rome, an office he held for almost two years until his election as General.

Father General Arrupe had become incapacitated and was clearly unable to carry on as General. In 1980 he, himself, had suggested that he resign and a Congregation be held to elect a successor.

On October 5, 1982 Pope John Paul II named Father Paolo Dezza as his Delegate—in effect, the Vicar General—to prepare for a Congregation to be held in the following autumn. So, on December 8, 1982 Dezza called for a Thirty-third General Congregation with the view of addressing two immediate problems: the resignation of Arrupe and the election of a new General. In addition, it was to treat of matters suggested by the Holy See.

It was to begin on the following September 1 and continue until October 25, 1983. The work of the Congregation began on September 2, 1983 and right away got down to the matters in hand. Before voting on Arrupe's resignation a eulogy on his exceptional life of devotion to the Society was given and, the delegates, then, voted secretly on the proposition. Arrupe's resignation was accepted forthwith by the assembled Fathers on September 3.

On the 13th the Fathers gathered in the chapel for an exhortation and a concelebrated Mass, after which a long time was spent in private prayer. In the Aula the Fathers gathered for the next session and Father Kolvenbach was elected General on the first ballot by an absolute majority of the votes. The result was quickly conveyed to the Pope who was on a pastoral visit in Austria.

Immediately after his election Father Kolvenbach's remarks to the delegates expressed the Society's profound gratitude to Father Arrupe for his sacrifice and long devotion to the Society, and to Father Dezza, the Pope's Delegate who had so successfully moved the Congregation along.

During the following years Father Kolvenbach carried on the example of Father Arrupe by visiting as many Jesuit Provinces and individual Jesuits as possible. As General his altruism and tranquility was displayed just as they had been when he was Provincial in the Near East in tempering of some misgivings of his subjects. As General his character has not changed from what it had been in the Near-East.

It was in September 1992 that he first issued the call for another Congregation. Then, on September 8, 1993, he fixed the dates of the 34th General Congregation to begin on January 5, 1995, and was to continue until March 22. It was to deal with the Mission of the Society in the world today, the Jesuit identity, as we perceive ourselves, and for a revision of laws to conform to the modern world updating the Society to conform to the new code of Canon Law. Possibly, he found himself frustrated by the precipitous drop in the numbers of Jesuits in the past twenty or thirty years and the few Jesuit Novices entering to replenish the ranks of the older members, who were slowly dying off, and being unable to stop the gradual out-flow. However, Father Kolvenbach's optimism was a continual encouragement to the members of the Society, which he conveyed by letter and numerous conferences as he visited the various provinces.

As of this writing Father Kolvenbach, God willing, still has years before him and will add to his many accomplishments and the many directives he has given for the future of the Company of Jesus and for the Greater Glory of God.

POSTLOGUE

Helas! As I put the last period to this work, I discover that a great doubt is hanging over those about whom these pages were written. Regarding the site of their internment, there is some question.

There are those of whom we have the facts, like Lainez and Borgia, whose relics were consumed (except for a few ashes) in the conflagration committed by a frenzied and fanatical mob in 1930 during the Communist regime in Spain. The Jesuit church in Madrid where their tombs were located was burned to the ground and left only a handful of ashes to remind us of Diego Lainez and Francisco de Borgia, former Generals of the Society of Jesus. Today, these ashes are immured in the present Jesuit church in Madrid on Avenida Maldonado.

Another, like Antonio Anderledy, who died in Fiesole near Florence, whose bones were interred initially in the parish church there, were later in the twentieth century re-interred in a common Jesuit ossuary in the Florence Municipal Cemetery where they rest among the fifty or so Jesuits who lived and died in the Florence area.

The four Vicars General of Poland are buried in their native country—known only to a few interested Poles. However, a few years ago two Polish Provinces produced an "Encyclopedia" of Jesuitica. It contains brief information of the four generals from "White Russia." This information is available in the *Encyklopedia, Wiedzy o Jezuitach Na Ziemiach Polski I Litwy 1564–1995*. Published by: Wydzial Filozoficzny, Towarzystwa Jesusowego, Instytut Kultury Religijnej, Wydawnictwo wam, Kraków, 1996.

As for the relics of our saintly founder, St. Ignatius de Loyola, there is some doubt as to whether his remains suffered the same fate as the other eighteen Fathers General who after their deaths were buried in the crypt of the Gesù Church. The missing relics of the Generals preceding the Suppression may be explained perhaps by the violence of the eighteenth and nineteenth centuries when marauding anticlerical soldiers pillaged churches, convents, and monasteries in search of loot and threw the unwanted relics into the street to be trampled to dust or thrown into the Tiber.

From the Restoration of the Society in 1814 until the present, the tombs of the Generals from Fortis to Janssens (except for Arrupe, who found his niche recently in the Pignatelli Chapel in the Gesù) are to be found in the mausoleum of the Jesuits in the Verano Cemetery on the eastern edge of Rome.

GENERALES S.J.

LOYOLA	1541–1556
LAINEZ	1558–1565
BORGIA	1565–1572
MERCURIAN	1573–1580
ACQUAVIVA	1581–1615
VITELLESCHI	1615–1645
CARAFFA	1646–1649
PICCOLOMINI	1649–1651
GOTTIFREDI	1652–1652 (2 months)
NICKEL	1652–1664
OLIVA	1664–1681
DE NOYELLE	1682–1686
GONZALEZ	1687–1705
TAMBURINI	1706–1730
RETZ	1730–1750
VISCONTI	1751–1755
CENTURIONE	1755–1757
RICCI	1758–1775
Czerniewicz	1782–1785 (White Russia)
Leinkiewicz	1785–1799 "
Kareu	1799–1802 "
Gruber	1802–1805 "
BRZOZOWSKI	1805–1820 (Poland)
FORTIS	1820–1829
ROOTHAAN	1829–1853
BECKX	1853–1887
ANDERLEDY	1887–1892
MARTIN	1892–1906
WERNZ	1906–1914
LEDOCHOWSKI	1915–1942
JANSSENS	1946–1964
ARRUPE	1965–1983
KOLVENBACH	1983–

SOURCES

Alvarez, Jaime, S.J. "Este Dia en la Compagnia de Jesus, 1995, Pasto, Colombia.

Bangert, William V., S.J. "History of the Society of Jesus" Second Edition. Revised and updated, 1986, Institute of Jesuit Studies, St. Louis.

Cassiani Ingoni, S.J., Guiliano, "P. Wlodimir Ledochowski, S.J. XXVI Generale della Compania di Gesu," 1945, Roma, Edizioni "La Civilta Cattolica", p. 376.

Documents of General Congregations 30 to 34.

Encilopedia Cattolica.

Gregorianum (1943) Universita Gregoriana, Roma.

Lamet, Pedro Miguel, "Arrupe," 1993, Ancora, Milano.

Lecouture, Jean, "Jesuites," 2 vol. une multibiographie, Editions du Seuil, 1992, Paris.

Memorias del Padre Luis Martin, S.J., General del Comp. De Jesus, 1988, Roma, IHSI.

New Catholic Encyclopedia.

Padberg, J., O'Keefe, M., McCarthy, J., "For Matters of Greater Moment, First Thirty General Congregations." Inst. Of Jesuit Studies, 1994, St. Louis.

Sommervogel, Carlos, "Bibliothèque de la Companie de Jesus," 1932, Sohepens, Louvain.

Schmitt, Ludovicus, S.J., "Synopsis Historia Societatis Jesu," Ratisbon, Pustet, 1914.

Portraits of the Generals are from the General Curia in Rome